There are only two places in the world where we can live happy: at home and in Paris.

- Ernest Hemingway -

WHITE STAR PUBLISHERS

The ancient churches of Paris are still in my memory. Their grandeur and their peacefulnes are unforgettable. The wonderful constructic of Notre Dame and the elaborate decoration with its beautiful sculptures cannot be forgotten. I felt then that those who expend millions on such divine cathedrals could not but have the love of God in their hearts.

- Mahatma Gandhi -

When spring comes to Paris
the humbles mortal alive must feel
that he dwells in paradise.

- Henry Miller -

I came to Paris, this divine city without God. We can't describe this, we must see how much beauty, how many beautiful things there are here, in the center of the world.

- Béla Bartók -

It is said that everything about Paris has already been written, and that with the books that have been written you could build a new Eiffel Tower.

– Mieczysław Kozłowski –

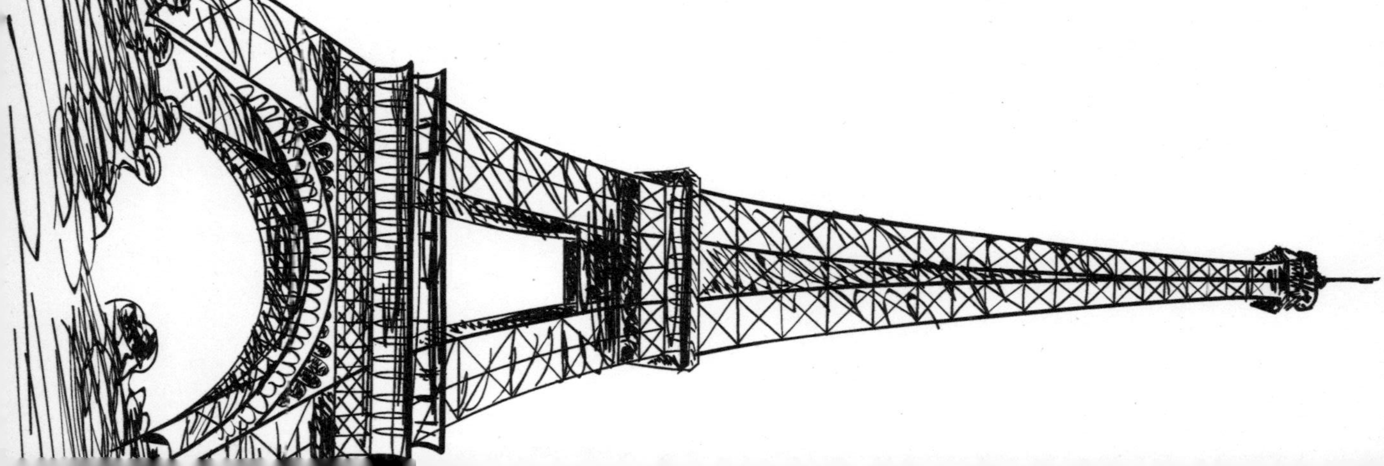

That Paris exists and anyone
could choose to live anywhere else
in the world will always be
a mystery to me!

- from the movie: Midnight in Paris -

Being a Parisian is not about being born in Paris, it is about being reborn there.

- Sacha Guitry -

CAFÉ

Living in Paris
was a crash course in chic.

- Rebecca Romijin -

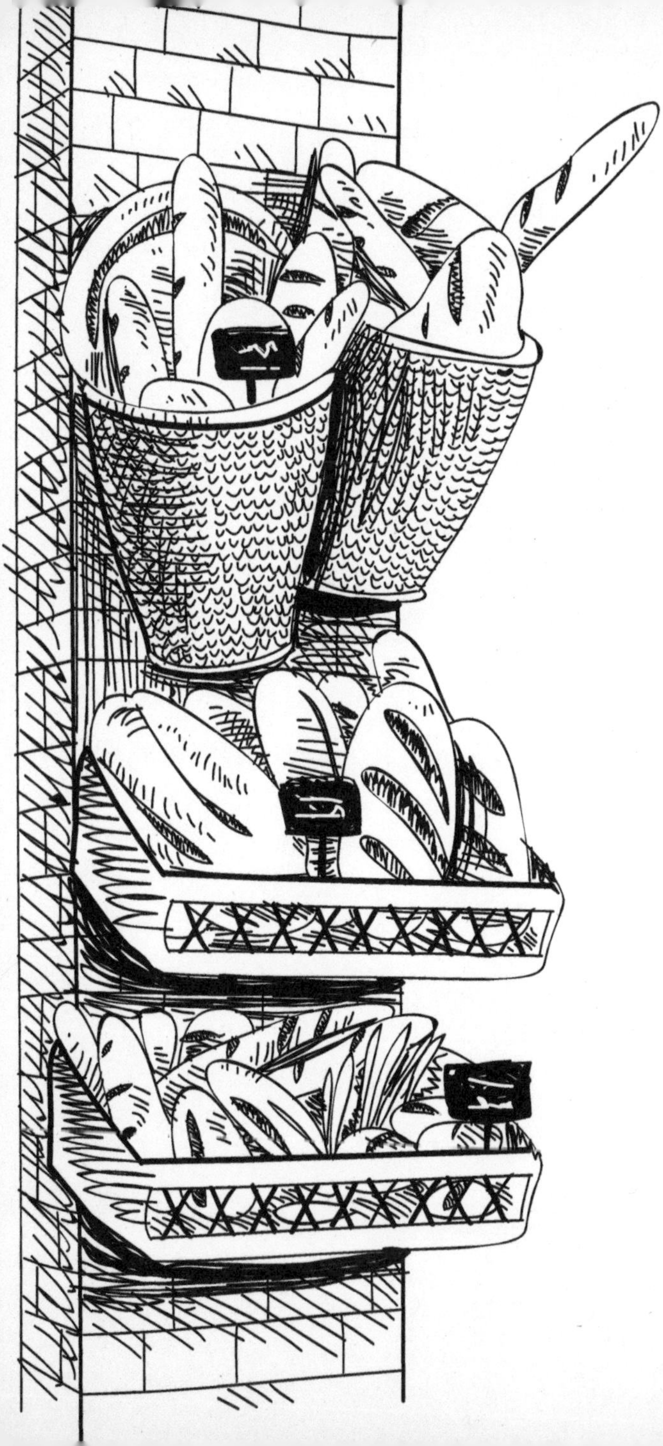

*Paris is a veritable ocean.
Take as many soundings in it
as you will, you will never know
its depth. Scour it and describe
it with the greatest care
you can, no matter how many
or how eager its explorers
may be, there will always be
some unknown cavern, some
flowers and pearls and monsters,
something unheard of, something
forgotten by the literary divers.*

– Honoré de Balzac –

A breath of Paris
preserves the soul.

- Victor Hugo -

I have before my eyes the twenty square miles where there have been the most thinking, writing and talking of the world.

– Jean Giraudoux –

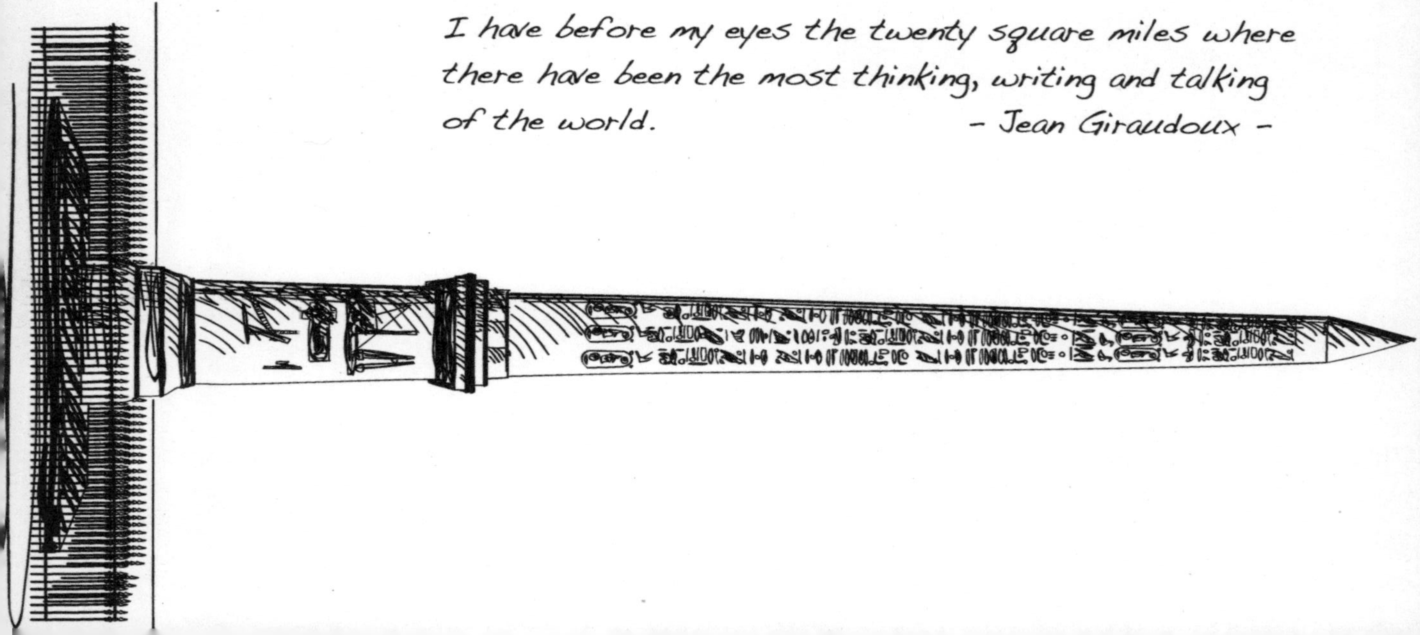

What an immense impression
Paris made upon me
It is the most extraordinary
place in the world.

- Charles Dickens -

BAZAR DE L'HOTEL DE VILLE

If God exists, I'm sure
he spends most of his time
at the Musée du Louvre.

- Joann Sfar -

In Paris we shall put out our soul's thirst for beautiful things created by famous artists. In Paris we shall visit the Panthéon and stop for a few minutes by the tombs of Victor Hugo, Rousseau, Chateaubriand, and Renan. In Paris we shall meander around the Palace of the Louvre and look upon the paintings of Raphael, Michelangelo, and Da Vinci. In Paris we shall go to the Opera and hear songs and hymns unveiled by the deity to Beethoven, Wagner, Mozart, and Rossini . . . These names, whose pronunciation is quite difficult to an Arabic-speaking person, are names of great men who founded the civilization of Europe; these are the names of men whom the earth has swallowed, but whose deeds it could not fold or cover. The tempest is capable of wasting the flowers but unable to harm the seeds.

– Kahlil Gibran –

A walk about Paris will provide lessons in history, beauty, and in the point of Life.

- Thomas Jefferson -

Paris is a place where, for me, just walking down a street that I've never been down before is like going to a movie or something. Just wandering the city is entertainment.

- Wes Anderson -

Paris is such a romantic place that even going to get a sandwich becomes a magic and unique moment.

- Kate Hudson -

When you embrace with one
glance the bright banks of the
Seine, the gardens, monuments,
and the immense and scattered
crowd coming from the bridges,
boulevards, copses, quays,
theaters, and flock confusedly
from every side of the square;
in that strange light, among
the spurts and falls of silvery
water, amid the statues, gigantic
candelabra, pillars and verdure,
in the limpid and perfumed air of
a beautiful summer night, then you
feel all the beauty of that spot,
inimitable in the whole world,
and you cannot refrain from crying,
Oh, Paris! Cursed and dear Paris!
Bold Siren, is it true that
one must flee you like a fury,
or adore you like a Goddess?

– Edmondo De Amicis –

METRO

This is what you do on your very first day in Paris. You get yourself, not a drizzle, but some honest-to-goodness rain, and you find yourself someone really nice and drive her through the Bois de Boulogne in a taxi. The rain's very important. That's when Paris smells its sweetest. It's the damp chestnut trees.

- Audrey Hepburn -

An artist has no home
in Europe
except in Paris.

- Friedrich Nietzsche -

In every rainbou
in Paris one can see
a triumphal arch

- Mieczysław Kozłowski -

When you want to explore new gastronomic frontiers, looking for creativity for new dishes you often go to Norway, to Spain, to England, but before reaching one of these Countries, it's necessary to stop in Paris. This city is a mix of traditions and of absolute culinary knowledge.

- Alessandro Borghese -

*Paris is the city in which one
loves to live. Sometimes
I think this is because it is
the only city in the world where
you can step out of a railway
station – the Gare d'Orsay –
and see, simultaneously,
the chief enchantments: the Seine
with its bridges and bookstalls,
the Louvre, Notre Dame,
the Tuileries Gardens, the Place
de la Concorde, the beginning
of the Champs Elysées –
nearly everything except the
Luxembourg Gardens and
the Palais-Royal. But what
other city offers as much
as you leave a train?*

– Margaret Anderson –

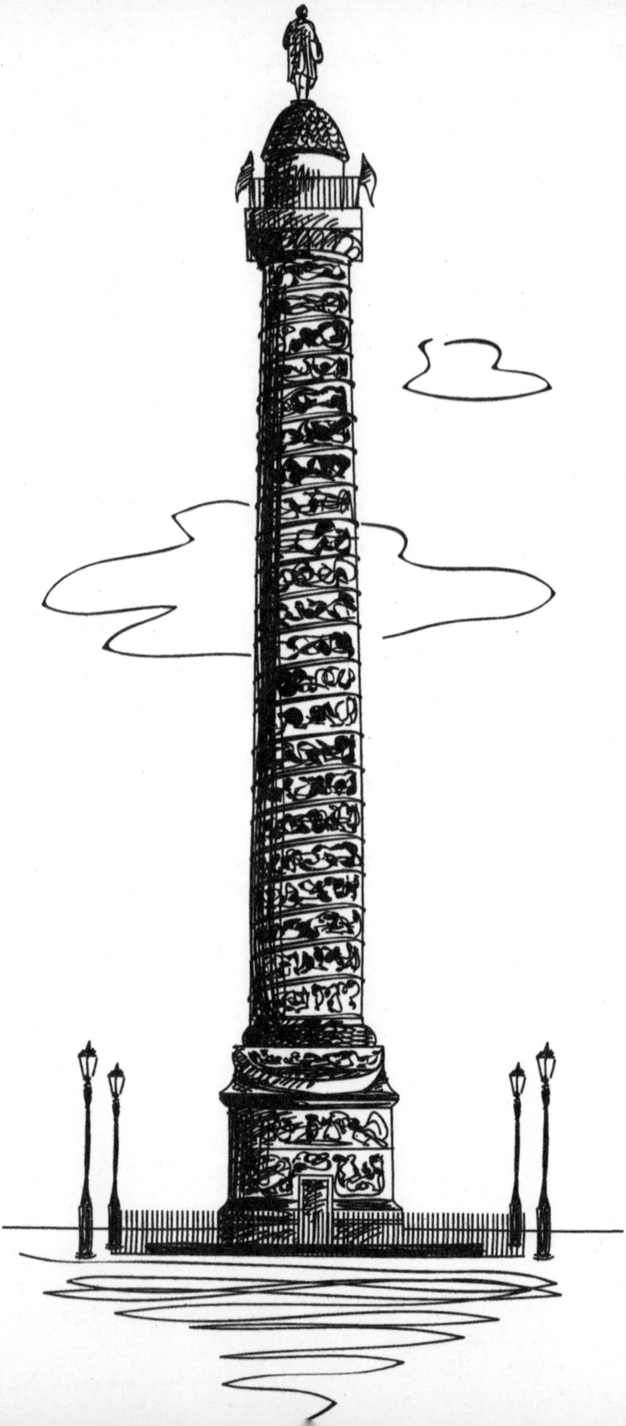

Saving Paris is more than saving
France, it's saving the world.
Paris is the centre of humanity
itself, Paris is the holy city.
If you attack Paris, you attack
the whole human race.

– Victor Hugo –

London is a riddle.
Paris is an explanation.

- G.K. Chesterton -

Add three letters to Paris
and it's paradise.

- Jules Renard -

If you are lucky enough
to have lived in Paris
as a young man, then wherever
you go for the rest of your
life it stays with you,
for Paris is a moveable feast.

- Ernest Hemingway -

Anderson, Margaret, *1886-1973, American writer*

Anderson, Wes, *1969-, American film director, film producer, screenwriter*

Balzac, Honoré de *1799-1850, French writer, playwright and essayist*

Bartók, Béla, *1881- 1945, Hungarian composer, pianist and ethnomusicologist*

Borghese, Alessandro, *1976-, Italian cook and anchor man*

Chesterton, G.K., *1874-1936, British writer, journalist and aphorist*

De Amicis, Edmondo, *1846-1908, Italian writer and journalist*

Dickens, Charles, *1812-1870, British writer, journalist and travel writer*

Gibran, Kahlil, *1883-1931, Lebanese poet and philosopher*

Giraudoux, Jean, *1882-1944, French writer and playwright*

Guitry, Sacha, *1885-1957, French actor, writer and screenwriter*

Hemingway, Ernest, *1899-1961, American writer and journalist*

Hepburn, Audrey, *1929-1993, British actress*

Hudson, Kate, *1979-, American actress and singer*

Hugo, Victor, *1802-1885, French writer, poet, playwright and politician*

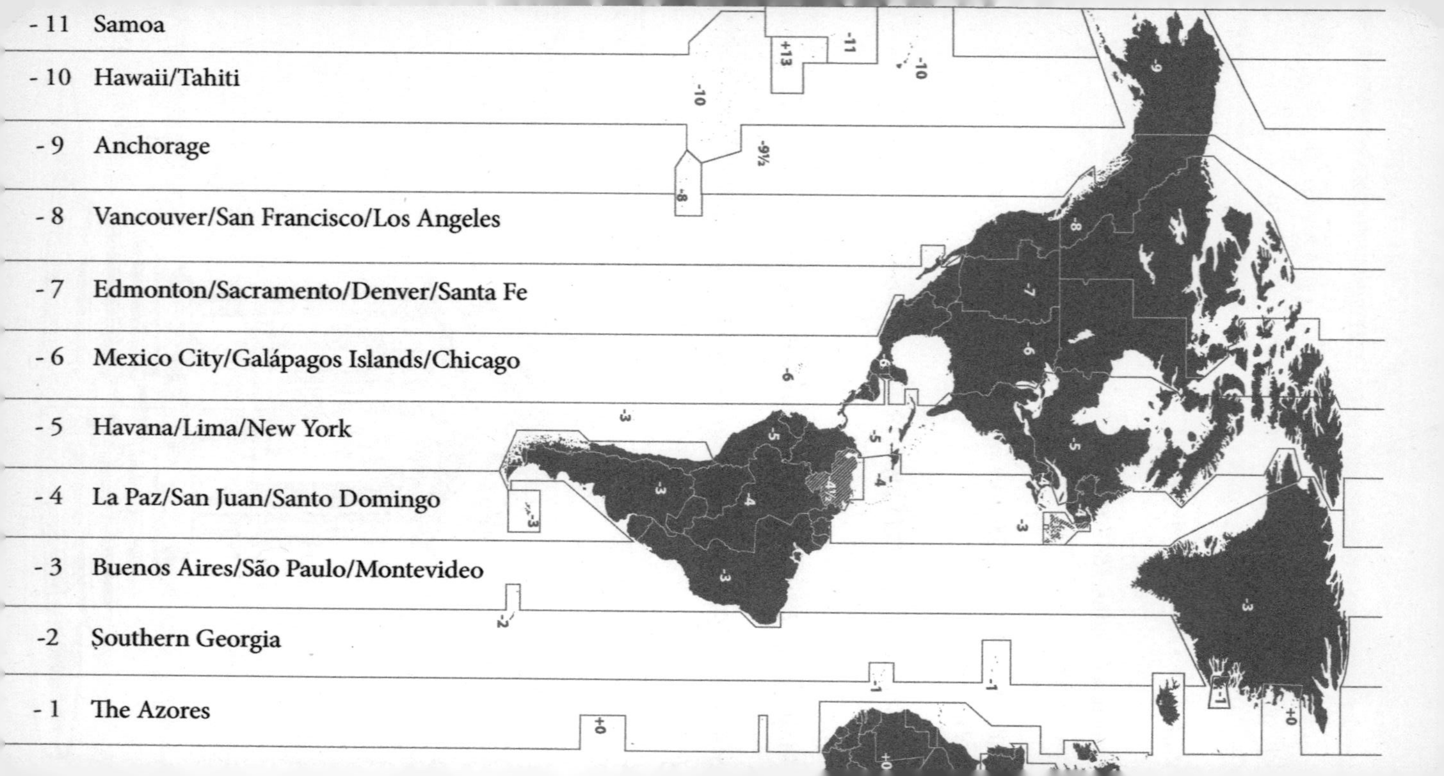
- 11 Samoa
- 10 Hawaii/Tahiti
- 9 Anchorage
- 8 Vancouver/San Francisco/Los Angeles
- 7 Edmonton/Sacramento/Denver/Santa Fe
- 6 Mexico City/Galápagos Islands/Chicago
- 5 Havana/Lima/New York
- 4 La Paz/San Juan/Santo Domingo
- 3 Buenos Aires/São Paulo/Montevideo
-2 Southern Georgia
- 1 The Azores

TIME ZONES

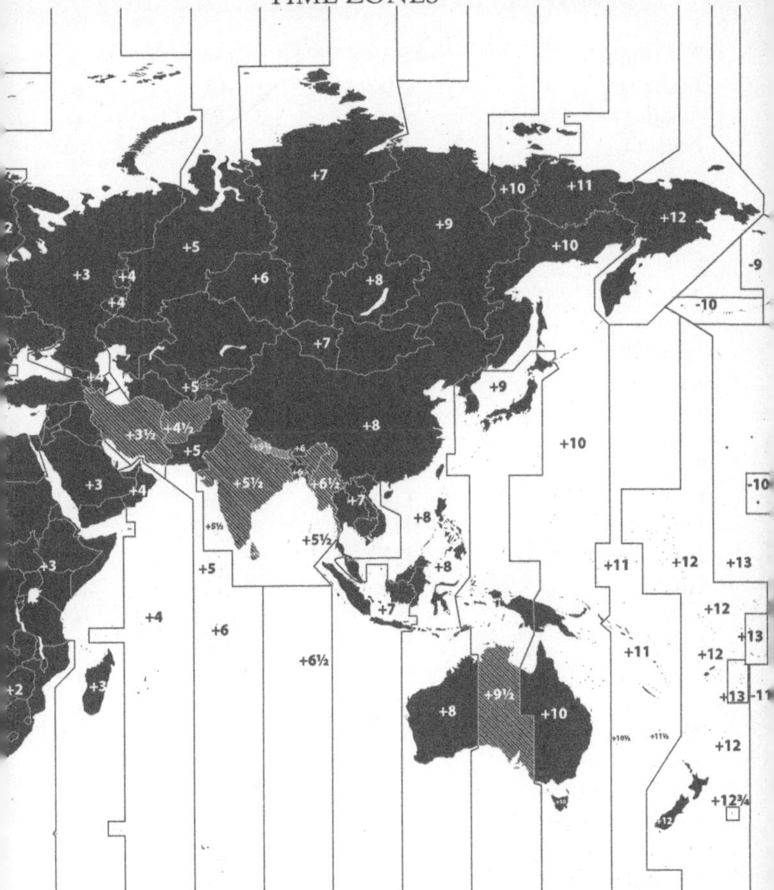

+ 2 Helsinki/Cairo/Bucharest/Cape Town

+ 3 Baghdad/Moscow/Nairobi

+ 4 Dubai/Abu Dhabi/Muscat

+ 5 Islamabad/Karachi/Tashkent

+ 6 Astana/Dhaka

+ 7 Bangkok/Hanoi/Jakarta

+ 8 Beijing/Hong Kong/Singapore/Taipei

+ 9 Osaka/Tokyo/Seoul

+ 10 Canberra/Melbourne/Sydney/Hobart

+ 11 Solomon Islands/Vanuatu Islands

+ 12 Auckland/Fiji

LICENSE PLATES, AREA CODES, DOMAINS,

Argentina	RA	+54	.ar
Australia	AUS	+61	.au
Austria	A	+43	.at
Belgium	B	+32	.be
Brazil	BR	+55	.br
Canada	CDN	+1	.ca
China	CN	+86	.cn
South Korea	ROK	+82	.kr
Croatia	HR	+385	.hr
Denmark	DK	+45	.dk
Finland	FIN	+358	.fi
France	F	+33	.fr
Germany	D	+49	.de
Japan	J	+81	.jp
Greece	GR	+30	.gr
Hong Kong	HK	+852	.hk
India	IND	+91	.in
Ireland	IRL	+353	.ie
Iceland	IS	+354	.is
Israel	IL	+972	.il
Italy	I	+39	.it
Malaysia	MAL	+60	.my
Mexico	MEX	+52	.mx
Norway	N	+47	.no
New Zealand	NZ	+64	.nz
The Netherlands	NL	+31	.nl
Poland	PL	+48	.pl
Portugal	P	+351	.pt
United Kingdom	GB	+44	.uk
Romania	RO	+40	.ro
Russia	RUS	+7	.ru
Slovakia	SK	+421	.sk
Slovenia	SLO	+386	.si
United States of America	USA	+1	.us
South Africa	ZA	+27	.za
Spain	E	+34	.es
Sweden	S	+46	.se
Switzerland	CH	+41	.ch
Turkey	TR	+90	.tr
Hungary	H	+36	.hu

LANGUAGES AND CURRENCY

Spanish	Argentine peso
English	Australian dollar
German	Euro
French (Walloon), Dutch (Flemish) and German	Euro
Portuguese	Brazilian real
English and French	Canadian dollar
Chinese	Chinese renminbi
Korean South	Korean won
Croatian	Croatian kuna
Danish	Danish krone
Finnish and Swedish	Euro
French	Euro
German	Euro
Japanese	Japanese yen
Greek	Euro
Chinese and English	Hong Kong dollar
Hindi and English	Indian rupee
Irish Gaelic and English	Euro
Icelandic	Icelandic króna
Hebrew and Arabic	New shekel
Italian	Euro
Malay	Malaysian ringgit
Spanish	Mexican peso
Norwegian	Norwegian krone
English and Māori	New Zealand dollar
Dutch and Frisian	Euro
Polish	Polish złoty
Portuguese	Euro
English	Pound sterling
Romanian	Romanian leu
Russian	Russian ruble
Slovak	Euro
Slovene, Italian and Hungarian	Euro
English	United States dollar
English and Afrikaans	South African rand
Spanish	Euro
Swedish	Swedish krona
German, French, Italian and Romansh	Swiss franc
Turkish	New Turkish lira
Hungarian	Hungarian Forint

Men

Shirts

USA	14½	15	15½	16	16½	17
GB	14½	15	15½	16	16½	17
D	37	38	39	40	41	42
F	37	38	39	40	41	42
I	37	38	39	40	41	42

Suits/Coats

USA	36	38	40	42	44	46
GB	36	38	40	42	44	46
D	40	42	44	46	48	50
F	42	44	46	48	50	52
I	46	48	50	52	54	56

Jeans

USA	32	33	34	35	36	38
GB	32	33	34	35	36	38
D	32	33	34	35	36	38
F	32	33	34	35	36	38
I	32	33	34	35	36	38

Shoes

USA	8½	9	9½	10	10½	11
GB	8	8½	9	9½	10	10½
D	40	41	42	43	44	45
F	40	41	42	43	44	45
I	40	41	42	43	44	45

Length

1 in = 2.54 cm
0.3937 in = 1 cm
1 SM = 1.6093 km
0.6214 SM = 1 km
1 NM = 1.8519 km
0.5400 NM = 1 km

Area

1 ac = 0.4047 ha
2.471 ac = 1 ha
1 SM^2 = 2.5900 km^2
0.3861 SM^2 = 1 km^2